D0562053

Nutri Ninja
Recipe Book

70 Smoothie Recipes for Weight Loss, Energy and Improved Health

By

Liana Green

Nutri Ninja Recipe Book

Disclaimer

This book is not intended as a substitute for the medical advice of physicians. The reader should regularly consult a physician in matters relating to his/her health and particularly with respect to any symptoms that may require diagnosis or medical attention.

Although the author and publisher have made every effort to ensure that the information in this book was correct at press time, the author and publisher do not assume and hereby disclaim any liability to any party for any loss, damage, or disruption caused by errors or omissions, whether such errors or omissions result from negligence, accident, or any other cause.

This book has no affiliation with Euro-Pro Operating LLC (the company that sells the Nutri Ninja) and is intended as a supplement to the Nutri Ninja Pro Blender.

Copyright © 2015 by Liana Green

All rights reserved. This book or any portion thereof may not be reproduced or used in any manner whatsoever without the express written permission of the publisher except for the use of brief quotations in a book review.

Introduction

Despite our best intentions, I know that we, as a family, do not consume enough nutrients in our daily diet. Since we have bought our blender, we have been experimenting with a variety of drinks, including ingredients that we simply wouldn't dream of incorporating into our regular mealtimes.

With smoothies we can include a wide range of fruits and vegetables. Eating plenty of colourful fruits and vegetables ensures we are getting the best nutritional combination of antioxidants, vitamins and minerals.

By making a healthy smoothie a part of our daily routine, my health, and my family's health, has improved in so many ways:

- My skin has become a lot clearer
- My hair feels healthier and looks shinier

- The whites of my eyes are much 'whiter'

- When I hit my afternoon slump, instead of drinking a cup of coffee and scoffing some biscuits, I am drinking a smoothie to energize myself.

- I am sleeping much better.

- I feel stronger - I am training for a marathon and have incorporated some of these recipes into my daily diet for an added nutrient boost.

- I feel much brighter - that is, my head feels clearer now that I am not relying on sugar for my energy highs.

- The children are consuming more than enough of their daily recommended fruit and vegetable intake. More importantly, they are enjoying it.

- My cravings for sugar and 'junk' food have dramatically reduced, resulting in weight loss.

Although shop bought smoothie drinks are convenient, they are often expensive and not as healthy as the ones you can make yourself at home. You can decide exactly what you put in your own drink and by drinking it when it is fresh, you can be sure you are getting maximum benefit from the vitamins and nutrients within it.

What This Book Can Do For You

You will find a selection of healthy yet delicious recipes to inspire you to make consuming raw fruit and vegetables a part of your daily diet. Each section will come with some helpful tips and hints, together with a breakdown of the nutritional attributes of each recipe.

Which Blender Should You Use?

Blenders have come a long way in recent years, the level of power has significantly increased and the price tag reduced. This means you can blend a variety of fruits, vegetables, nuts and seeds in a convenient and cost effective manner.

The recipes in this book are aimed at all high power blenders. I personally have and use the Nutri Ninja Pro Blender (BL450) on a daily basis. But I know that these recipes can be used just as effectively in the Nutribullet. Both blenders are very similar in terms of what they can blend.

The Basics of Smoothie Making

Of course you purchased this book for recipe inspiration. However, it doesn't hurt to have an idea of the basics of smoothie making, and to know what combinations work well together.

There may be some ingredients in my recipes that you can either not get hold of where you live, or you really cannot stomach. For me, I have a mainly dislike relationship with celery. No matter how much I try and disguise it in a smoothie, it just keeps on shining through. So, instead of trying to force myself to drink it, I will just swap it out with something else.

Hopefully this guide will give you the confidence to play around with the recipes and experiment with some of your own creations.

If you loosely follow these pointers, you won't go far wrong.

The Smoothie Base Liquid

Depending on the ingredients you are using, most smoothies will require a liquid of some sort to make them a consistency that is pleasant to drink.

Water

I normally use water, mainly because I always have it in the house. Of course, water is fantastic for staying adequately hydrated and much cheaper than buying up lots of other liquids to blend. Be careful how much you add, if you add too much it will take away some of the taste of the smoothie.

Coconut Water

My second go to liquid base is coconut water. You may well have seen it taking up more shelf space at the local supermarket as the health benefits are becoming better known.

Not only does it taste great, it is also packed full of nutrients. In fact, coconut water contains magnesium, calcium, potassium, sodium and phosphorus. The five essential electrolytes found in the human body. The fat content of coconut water is very low, meaning you can drink it in the knowledge that not only is it doing you good, it is also not making you pile on the pounds.

Unsweetened Almond Milk

Almond milk is 100% plant based and rich in antioxidants. It is a great source of vitamin E which contributes to the protection of cells from oxidative stress. Not only that, almond milk is naturally low in fat and easy to digest due to it being naturally lactose free. The smooth, creamy and nutty taste will add to the taste of any smoothie.

As long as you use an almond milk that is unsweetened with no additives, it will be low in carbohydrates, meaning that by using it you won't significantly increase your blood sugar levels. Other benefits include being low in sodium with no cholesterol or saturated fat. It is high in the healthy fats, including omega fatty acids.

Almond milk is high in fibre, aiding the digestion of your smoothie.

Vitamins include iron and riboflavin which are necessary for muscle growth and healing.

Although almond milk only contains 1 gram of protein per serving, it contains plenty of B vitamins such as iron and riboflavin, both important for muscle growth and healing.

Chilled Green Tea

You can't have missed the hype surrounding the health benefits of green tea. And it is with good reason. It is rich in polyphenols and catechins that can help fight various cancers and help your heart function properly.

High Fibre Carbohydrates

When people talk about carbohydrates we often think of bread, pasta, potatoes etc. However, carbohydrates can be found in many plant-based foods. Carbohydrates often hit the headlines when diet and health is being discussed. They are frequently given a bad rap for making you put on weight.

However, if you are eating the right kinds of carbs they will provide you with plenty of health benefits and play a vital role in reaching your optimum health levels.

Not all carbohydrates are created equally, so swapping out the unhealthy unnatural ones for unprocessed or minimally processed plant-based foods, will provide you with essential fibres which may help protect you against a number of health conditions. These fibre rich carbohydrates will also leave you with a fuller feeling, meaning you aren't constantly craving snacks that might not be quite so good for you.

There are many high fibre carbohydrates that are good for you, some of which you will find in the following recipes. They include spinach, cucumber, kale, celery, apples, raspberries, blueberries, strawberries.

The Fruits and Vegetables

As I mention a few times in this book, the best ingredients you can put in your smoothie are the green leafy variety. Spinach, kale, romaine lettuce, watercress, whatever you have available. Even if you don't enjoy these and think they will ruin your smoothie, please give them a try. Start off with a little and gradually build up. As you taste buds adjust you will want to include more, especially once you begin to notice the health benefits of consuming them.

When picking which fruits and vegetables to use, a great rule of thumb is to go colourful.

Experiment with produce that is red, green, purple, orange and yellow.

If you are able, freeze some of your fruits and vegetables. Chopped bananas, pineapple, melon, berries, grapes and other exotic fruits are great to just grab out of the freezer and pop in your blender.

Many of the smoothie recipes in this book are suitable for freezing and turning into ice lollies. The perfect nutrient rich and healthy pudding, that actually tastes good.

Healthy Fats

By adding some healthy fats to your smoothie you will fill fuller for longer, feel more energized and benefit from the extra nutrients and vitamins included in those ingredients.

What healthy fats can you include? My favourite that I like to use is avocado. Adding avocado will make the smoothie quite a bit thicker so you may want to add more liquid. If you don't like the taste of avocados very much you can easily mask it with some raspberries, strawberries or a ripe banana.

Avocados are incredibly nutritious and come with many health benefits. They are very high in potassium (more so than a banana). Avocados are incredibly high in monounsaturated oleic acid, a "heart healthy" fatty acid that is believed to be one of the main reasons for the health benefits of olive oil. Avocados also have a lot of fibre in them which as we know is great for filling fuller. It will also benefit our digestive system.

Nuts and seeds are another brilliant addition to a smoothie. In particular, as the Nutri Ninja (and the Nutri bullet if you are using one instead) is such a powerful machine, they can be blended up to a very smooth consistency, which for some people means they are easier to consume.

Most of us don't eat nearly enough seeds and nuts. They are incredibly healthy and are packed full of fibre, fat, protein, minerals and vitamins.

The best way to decide which nuts and seeds to eat is to eat a variety of them. Many supermarkets and health shops sell mixed bags so you can throw a handful of these into a smoothie.

Nuts I like to include are almonds, Brazil nuts, almonds, walnuts, pecans and cashews.

For seeds I tend to use a mix of sesame, flax, sunflower, pumpkin and chia.

Each of these nuts and seeds bring an amazing amount of health benefits and I really encourage you to try and add some to your smoothies.

This is my favourite one. Chocolate. High quality dark chocolate has been proven in scientific studies to be a great antioxidant, and rich in healthy fats. Try and choose an organic one that is high in cocoa content (70-90%). You will find some yummy recipes which include dark chocolate.

Proteins

By adding protein rich ingredients to your smoothies you will help curb your hunger pangs as well as aid tissue repair, build lean muscle (which helps you burn more fat,) and provide you with more energy.

You may choose to get your proteins from a manufactured powder which you simply stir into your smoothie. I don't use protein powders so couldn't comment on which ones are better than others, I just try to use natural ingredients from foods to get my protein intake.

Here are some of my preferred protein sources to use in smoothies;

Unsweetened almond milk, coconut milk, flax seeds, oats, chia seeds, soya milk.

There are of course many more and it depends on your tastes and what is available locally for you.

Why Drink Smoothies?

Do you feel tired, over weight or simply have no zest for life? The old saying of we are what we eat, has never been truer. The Western world is facing unprecedented levels of obesity, diabetes and other serious health problems.

You can do something about it. And the good news? It doesn't have to be hard. You don't (and shouldn't) need to deprive yourself of food to be healthy. It is perfectly ok to eat enough food to feel full, as long as it is the right kind of food. The other goods news; it doesn't have to turn your life upside down. You can add as little as one smoothie a day, and combined with other healthy eating choices you will soon begin to see the differences.

Drinking Smoothies for Improved Health

We all know that the best solution for good health is prevention. Unfortunately this isn't always possible. We all go through periods of our lives when we are not taking good enough care of our bodies. Or perhaps you are, and you've just been unlucky and developed an ailment despite your best intentions. Whatever the reason, by drinking at least a smoothie a day, you can help alleviate your problem and give your body the best chance of fighting the problem.

Smoothies are a fantastic choice for staying hydrated. Fruits and vegetables contain large amounts of water. The human body is made up of roughly 60 per cent water and we need to make sure we stay well hydrated, especially if you are active.

Smoothies for Weight Loss

Yes, smoothies can be used to aid you in weight loss. But it is important to make sure you are drinking the right combination to ensure that you are not denying your body of the vitals nutrients for full health. I go in to more details in the chapter dedicated to weight loss, suggesting how you might lose weight and improve your health with the right selection of ingredients.

Using Your Nutri Ninja Blender

Using your blender is fairly straight forward, which is the beauty of it. However, it is worth being aware of a few basics so that you can use your blender to its full potential and avoid any pitfalls.

You can prepare a wide array of wholesome recipes, including smoothies, sauces, soups and meals. Although this book purely focuses on smoothies, future books will cover the other types of recipes. The variety of different food types you can use is what makes this blender so versatile.

Order of Ingredients

It is important to put the easier to blend items in first followed by the harder to blend items. So, for example, in our Green Machine Smoothie recipe you would put the spinach in first, followed by avocado, cucumber, pineapple and then finally the ice cubes. Then top up with your liquid. This way when you connect the cup to the blade section the ice cubes are at the bottom by the blades, making it easier to blend to a smooth consistency.

What Can I Put In?

You can put most things in the blender without the need to take out the pips or seeds, with the exception of the following;

Apples seeds, apricot stones, cherry stones, plum stones, peach stones, avocado stones.

Once you have been through a few of our recipes and are feeling a bit more confident, you can experiment with different ingredients and measurements. There are no strict rules on what you put with what, other than what your taste buds might think of it!

As a basic rule of thumb though, I would follow these combination guidelines;

50% Leafy Greens

(Kale, Spinach, Spring Greens, Romaine Lettuce, Swiss Chard)

50% Fruit

(Apples, Carrots, Bananas, Berries etc)

Optional Boost

I like to add an extra nutrient boost to my smoothies, these can be seeds, nuts, ground flaxseed, goji berries, acai berries etc

---

Liquid

Fill the Nutri Ninja cup to the max line with a liquid of your choice (water, coconut water, unsweetened nut milks, soya milk etc)

Using Frozen Ingredients

Where we can, we tend to use frozen fruits. Especially blueberries, strawberries, pineapple, mango and bananas. Not only does this mean we can use them year round, it also means we don't need to add extra ice cubes.

If you don't or can't get the frozen variety, you can chop them up as soon as you have bought them and store them in bags in the freezer. Of course if you would prefer to just use them as you buy them fresh, just pop in some ice cubes to get a nice smooth and cold drink. Due to the amazing power of the Nutri Ninja Blender, you can easily blend ice cubes and any frozen fruits and vegetables.

Smoothie Consistency

Depending on how you like the consistency of your smoothie you may want to adjust the recipes slightly. The following ingredients will make your drink thicker or thinner so you can get it tasting just how you like it:

Thinner

Water

Coconut water

Green Tea (chilled)

Unsweetened nut milks

Thicker

Avocado

Ripe banana

Chia Seeds

Oatmeal

Making it Sweet

If you are used to drinking sweeter smoothies it may take a while to adjust your taste buds. To make it easier on yourself why not try adding some of the following sugar alternatives. It is really important not to add refined sugar. The less processed a sugar is, the better it is for you.

- Raw honey
- Dried fruits such as dates, dried figs, raisins and apricots
- Maple syrup (natural)

We mainly add honey when we feel like a bit of extra sweetness in our smoothies.

Blending It

Once all your chosen ingredients are in the cup, screw the blade part on to the cup and fix it to the motor part of the Nutri Ninja.

This is where the Nutri Ninja is a game changer for us. It will blend your ingredients into a really smooth drink, no chunks or seedy bits floating around.

It shouldn't need more than 30 seconds of blending to get the desired consistency.

If you want to, you can drink it straight from the cup. Or pour some out into a glass and store the rest in the fridge by putting the supplied lid on top.

> **TIP:** Don't overfill the cup. Don't go past the marked out max line, this may result in you breaking the seal and the smoothie leaking in the future.

Should You Buy Organic Food?

Once upon a time everything was eaten in season and grown in naturally fertilized soils. Now, as we all know, fields are sprayed with pesticides, herbicides and fungicides. The demand for out of season fruits and vegetables has meant that products are often picked before they are ripe so that they can be transported to reach the supermarket shelves in all corners of the world. By which time much of the nutritional value has dramatically reduced.

Buying organic produce is always the better option, if you are able to, due to the sustainable way in which it is grown, without pesticides, preservatives or artificial ingredients. However, it isn't always possible to buy organic, whether it is due to financial reasons (it is more expensive) or it simply isn't readily available where you live.

Where possible, I try to use local organic produce. Of course this is not always feasible, and in these cases I will use the next best thing. For example, if I want to add blueberries and they are not in season, I will buy some frozen blueberries. In fact, frozen fruits are fantastic to put in smoothies. A cold smoothie tastes yummy and the convenience of just grabbing it out of the freezer will mean you make and consume way more smoothies.

If you are only able to buy a few organic items then the following are the ones you should make priority;

Apples

Strawberries

Grapes

Celery

Peaches

Spinach

Cucumbers

Kale

Pineapples

Soft Citrus

Carrots

If you are unsure of the origin always follow these guidelines;

- Peel non organic hard fruits and vegetables before blending or wash very thoroughly.

- Wash all berries before blending.

- Remove skins of citrus fruits that may have been waxed.

Tips for a Healthy Lifestyle

Stay Hydrated

Try to drink at least 8 glasses of water each day. If you drink a glass when you think you are hungry this will help determine if you are really hungry or just dehydrated. Drinking more water can help speed up your metabolism. Water helps blood transport oxygen and other important nutrients around your body. Water will help you when you work out, not only to stay hydrated, but to keep your joints lubricated. Drinking water can also help keep your skin hydrated and younger looking. Flushing out all those toxins can only be a good think for creating your outer glow!

Keep a Food Journal

By keeping a daily food diary you can see the times of day when you are slipping into bad habits. For example, I know that the evenings are a hard time for me. I am used to snacking whilst I'm writing or watching a film. Pre-empt this time by preparing a smoothie or healthy snack in advance.

Healthy Snacks on Standby

Keep healthy quick bites nearby. A handful of seeds and nuts or some raw carrots or cucumber to dip into some yummy hummus. Carry some fruit with you when you are out and about so you are not tempted to duck into the supermarket for a quick treat.

Take Regular Exercise

Find something that *you* enjoy doing. Go for a walk, run, cycle, swim, or whatever makes you happy. Mix it up and combine a variety of exercises. Get friends and family involved, join clubs. Not only will exercise help create a healthy lifestyle physically, it will help your mind.

Go Natural

Swap the processed food for natural. The less human intervention it has had the better. Hopefully, once you have integrated a smoothie or 2 into your daily diet, you will start to lean towards the more natural foods anyway.

Eat a Balanced Diet

Make sure you are getting enough of each food. Keep them as 'clean' and natural as possible. Be sure to include lean proteins, fibre, healthy fats and good carbohydrates. Protein will help you feel full for longer periods of time. What's more, protein will help you build and keep muscle mass. Muscle naturally burns more calories than fat. So don't forget the protein! Good sources of protein include chicken, salmon, turkey and lean steak.

Get Enough Sleep

It is easy to skip on sleep. And not always through choice! We all need differing amounts of sleep but I know when I haven't had enough I am cranky, tired and reaching for the nearest energy boost. Of course, if you have unavoidably missed out on your zzz's then try and get more energy with an extra smoothie rather than junk food.

Treat Yourself

Look after yourself. Treat yourself to things that make you feel great. Whether it's a massage, a spa day, a new hair cut or a new outfit, reward yourself for improving your health. Leading a healthy lifestyle is a package, nutrition plays a huge part in it but so do other factors. Look after the whole of you.

The Recipes

The bit you are waiting for, getting stuck into making your smoothies. I have tried where possible to split the smoothie recipes into chapters according to their health benefits. Of course there is a lot of overlap between chapters, and what I recommend most of all is to switch it up each day as much as your ingredients will allow. Variety of raw food is the key to a healthy you.

Each recipe measurements are based on using the larger cup size (24oz). This cup size generally makes 2 large drinks or 3 small ones (depending on how much you want to drink of course!) If you want to make less then just reduce the recipes accordingly.

Remember, if you want to make a smoothie thinner then add some more liquid, or if you prefer a thicker consistency add ice or some extra ingredients like banana, avocado, chia seeds etc.

My measurements do not need to be followed precisely, which is why I have used 'handfuls' quite a bit throughout the recipes. Don't get too caught up in the exact quantities, use that time to get blending and drinking. Use mine as a rough guide. For example, if I say 2 handfuls of spinach and 1 handful of mixed berries, you know you need to use roughly twice the amount of spinach as berries.

A lot of the smoothie recipes include kale, spinach or another kind of leafy green. This is because greens are the powerhouse of nutrition. They are packed with proteins, antioxidants, vitamins and a variety of other benefits your body needs. Where you see a green leafy ingredient, please feel free to substitute it for what you have available. For example, if it says spinach, feel free to swap it for kale, or romaine lettuce or mixed spring greens etc. Rotate them round as much as possible so that you can gain the different nutritional benefit from each ingredient.

Most of all, enjoy creating your smoothies and reaping the rewards of a healthy new you!

Smoothie Recipes for Weight Loss

Whether you want to lose a few pounds or a lot of pounds, you will be pleased to know that smoothies can help you. Not only can you make some fabulous tasting ones, you will also fuel your body with an incredible array of nutrients, vital for a healthy lifestyle.

Many people like to know how many calories they are consuming when they are trying to lose weight. Personally I don't like to do this as it kind of takes the fun out of eating. For instance, if adding half an avocado would take me over a recommended calorie meal allowance, I certainly wouldn't leave it out. The reason being is that avocados, whilst high in fat, they are high in the fat that is incredibly good for you!

Making Smoothies a Daily Habit

In my opinion, it makes sense to start on your road to healthy and wholesome eating by making smoothie drinking a daily habit. Pick some smoothies from this book and plan your food for the week ahead. Make sure you have the necessary ingredient and write out which smoothies you are going to have and when.

If you can, make them and consume them at the same time every day. For me, this is first thing in the morning, right after I have had a glass of cold water (the best way to start the day!) Do this EVERY single day without fail. Even if you are missing an ingredient, still make it. Or you don't think you fancy a smoothie, still make it. It will make you feel amazing for the day.

After a while of drinking a healthy smoothie each day you will start to notice that you don't necessarily crave the other junk and processed food so much.

Losing Weight with Smoothies

If you want to lose weight then why not try and swap one of your meals for a smoothie? For me, this would be breakfast, I make a smoothie big enough that it will last me for a mid-morning guzzle too. Or have a smoothie for breakfast and lunch and then eat a healthy and wholesome meal at dinner time.

Only eat whole foods that have no added nasties in them. Opt for wholegrain where you can and still pile up the vegetables on your plate. If you feel hungry in the day then snack on healthy foods. Raw fruit and vegetables or boiled eggs are just a few examples.

Go Easy on Yourself

Don't feel bad if you break this and end up scoffing a bag of crisps or a pizza - just get back on track the next day if you can. Personally, I think some people need this little leeway in their diet for 'forbidden foods' - I know I certainly do! Call it a 5 or 10% allowance. Just keep it balanced. Of course if you don't have the urge for the odd slice of cake or chocolate bar then no problem, don't go forcing yourself!

Ok, let's dive into the recipes then. As with all of them, feel free to chop them around according to your tastes and what ingredients you have available.

Berry Peachy

1 handful of kale

2 peaches

2 handfuls of frozen or fresh mixed berries

1 handful (or around 12) grapes

2 tablespoons of ground flaxseeds

Water

Making It

Wash all the ingredients. Chop the peaches. Put all of the ingredients in your Nutri Ninja and blend. Add water to maximum line or less if you prefer a thicker consistency.

Did You Know

Peaches are a great source of vitamins C and A. Peaches have a high water and fibre content which helps you to feel full for longer.

Ground flaxseeds contain many healthy fats and have a high fibre content. They can be added to a variety of foods, not just smoothies, try a table spoon sprinkled on cereal. Flaxseed contains a plant-based omega-3 fatty acid (linolenic acid) that helps to increase the feelings of being full.

Boost Me Up Ginger

1 carrot

1 pear

1 apple

1cm of fresh root ginger

250ml of coconut water (or plain water)

Ice cubes

Making It

Chop the apple and remove the seeds. Place all the ingredients in your blender. You may want to start off with a smaller amount of fresh root ginger if you are not use to consuming it raw in a smoothie. Build it up gradually until you are comfortable with the zingy taste. Adjust the liquid content to desired consistency.

Did You Know

Ginger can play an integral part in the weight loss process by acting as a fat burner. Ginger helps to raise your metabolism, meaning you burn more calories. It can also act as a natural appetite suppressant, making you feel fuller and less likely to overindulge.

Carrots have an abundance of health benefits. They are a low-calorie food that also provides essential dietary fibre. This is ideal for weight management as they will make you feel fuller for longer.

Apples and pears both have a high water content and high dietary fibre, again helping with making you feel full up without adding too many calories.

Needy Seedy

2 handfuls of spinach

8 frozen or fresh strawberries

1/2 frozen banana

250ml Coconut Water

2 Tbsp of Chia Seeds

Ice cubes

Making It

This makes for a great afternoon treat. Place all of the ingredients in your blender and whizz. Enjoy this delicious smoothie safe in the knowledge that it is good for you!

Did You Know

Chia Seeds are grown natively in Mexico. They were said to be the basic survival ration of the

Aztecs and Mayans. Chia seeds are super healthy as they are rich in healthy omega-3 fatty acids, antioxidants, protein, calcium, fibre and various micro nutrients. Aside from being a nutritional powerhouse, chia seeds act by expanding in size when in liquid. This means, if you drink your smoothie shortly after making it, the chia seeds will expand in your stomach, meaning you will feel much fuller for much longer. Chia seeds are 40% fibre by weight, meaning they are the best source of fibre in the world. If you are consuming chia seeds outside of a smoothie, make sure you are drinking adequate liquid (water) with them.

Bananas often get a bad rap for being high in calories. So why include them in a weight loss section? Well, bananas are filling, and as they are sweet in taste, they curb any sugar cravings you might be having. I like to snack on a ripe banana if I feel like an energy boost. A medium one is only around 100 calories, that's the same as some biscuits! I know which one will work better with my waistline and keep me feeling fuller for longer!

Strawberries are said to speed up your metabolic rate by helping to promote the production of certain fat burning hormones. Aside from the amount of antioxidants that these delicious berries contain, they also have enough fibre to help with your digestion. Strawberries make for another great snacking food. I especially like them in the evening after dinner.

Green Tea Smoothie

1 handful of frozen blueberries

1 banana

1 pinch of cinnamon

200ml chilled green tea

Ice cubes

Making It

Make the required amount of green tea and allow it to chill enough to put in the Nutri Ninja. Add all the remaining ingredients and blend for 30 seconds.

Did You Know

Green tea not only has the benefit of boosting metabolism, it is also thought to reduce bad cholesterol. It makes a brilliant base to a smoothie as it is so low in calories.

Cinnamon is a great way of improving the flavour of a smoothie, especially if you are trying to mask a taste you don't like, it can also leave you feeling fuller for longer and keeps blood sugar levels more balanced.

Blueberries are rich in nutritional value and full of powerful antioxidants, vitamin C and potassium. They contain no fat and low in calories. I tend to keep blueberries frozen (I either buy them frozen or put our own home grown ones straight in the freezer once we have picked them.) Blueberries are great for your digestive system due to the insoluble fibre they contain.

Chocolate Velvet

1 handful of kale

2 chunks of grated dark Chocolate (minimum 75% cocoa content)

1 frozen banana

200ml unsweetened almond milk (or any other nut milk/soy milk)

Ice Cubes

Making It

Place all ingredients in the Nutri Ninja and blend. Enjoy.

Shhh! Don't tell anyone we've sneaked a chocolate smoothie into a weight loss chapter! Who said losing weight had to be boring? Not I. If you enjoy chocolate please don't deny yourself of it when trying to lose weight. All that will happen, is you will crave it, you will initially resist it, and then you'll go crazy and reach for the nearest bar! Well, that's me anyway.

Did You Know

If you incorporate the best kind of **dark chocolate** into your diet, in moderation, you will not only satisfy that chocolate urge, you'll also be treating your body to some pretty amazing antioxidants. **Dark chocolate** (at least 75% cocoa) is very nutritious. Quality chocolate is actually rich in fibre, iron, magnesium amongst other minerals. So go on, enjoy it!

Red Hot Chilli Smoothie

Handful of frozen strawberries

1/2 red chilli pepper

1cm of fresh root ginger

1 cup of orange juice

Juice of half a lime

Water

Making It

Carefully chop up the chilli, removing the seeds. Maybe start with a smaller bit of chilli and taste the smoothie before adding more. Try and use freshly squeezed orange juice if you can. Put all the ingredients in and blend. Add water to make desired consistency. Go with me on this one. I know a **red chilli** in your smoothie might not sound quite right, but trust me, it does taste pretty good.

Did You Know

Chillis are a brilliant way to speed up your metabolism. Chilli peppers raise your endorphin level, making you feel pretty great. Chili peppers also have a compound in them call capsaicin which increases energy, acts as an appetite suppressant and boosts metabolism. Sometimes I'll add a little dark chocolate into the mix - try it, it is delicious. Just remember to handle those hot ones with care. Nothing worse than rubbing your eye when you've got hot spice on it. I've been there. Ouch.

Oh, Brussels

1 handful of spinach

3 brussel sprouts

1 apple

1/4 medium pineapple

Half a lime

250ml of coconut water

Ice cubes

Making It

If you are not a fan of the controversial sprout then maybe try with just 1 to start with and work your way up. Put all the ingredients in your Nutri Ninja and blend.

Did You Know

Ok, ok, I know. Brussel sprouts. I sense a little trepidation with this one. I almost got evicted from the house today when I revealed the ingredient in this little gem. Maybe I'm a little biased as I adore brussel sprouts, but this didn't actually taste too bad. **Brussel sprouts** have some incredible health benefits due to their antioxidants. Not only that, if you get them when they are in season, the sweet ones taste pretty good and are low in calories. Perfect for a weight loss smoothie. At least give it a try!

Go Green

1 handful of kale

1 handful of spinach

1 banana

1 apple

1 tbsp of ground flaxseeds

Water

Ice cubes

Making it

Place all ingredients into blender and blend until a smooth consistency. Add more water if desired.

Did You Know

Kale and spinach are popular choices when making a green smoothie. They are excellent sources of vitamin k which your body uses to help with bone development and keeping your blood healthy. By including 2 cups of raw spinach and (or) kale in your daily smoothie you will consume your recommended daily intake of vitamin K.

The high levels of vitamin A in both leafy greens also help to keep your skin clear by maintaining a healthy skin cell function.

I like to make this smoothie and have it for my breakfast.

Perfect Pears

2 handfuls of mixed spring greens

1 handful of frozen or fresh mixed berries

2 pears, chopped with the skin still on.

250ml of water

Making It

Put all ingredients in your blender and blend for 30 seconds. Add more water if required.

Did You know

The skin of a **pear** is said to contain about half of the pear's whole dietary fibre. The skin also contains many of the antioxidants of the pear. As pears are so fibrous they can really help with weight loss whilst providing important antioxidants and flavonoids.

Berries are also a great source of fibre, alongside other health benefits. For example, raspberries contain ketones which are said to prevent an increase in overall body fat. More importantly, berries taste fantastic and can really sweeten up a smoothie.

The Raspberry Rush

2 handfuls of spinach

1 banana

1 handful of fresh or frozen raspberries

Water

Ice cubes

Making It

Place all the ingredients in your Nutri Ninja cup. I prefer to use frozen raspberries so that I can use them year round. Blend and add more water (or other liquid) as required.

Did You Know

Raspberries have a lot going for them. Not only do they taste delicious, they are also packed full to the brim with nutrients, vitamins and minerals. They are low in fat and calories, but rich in dietary fibre and antioxidants.

Tropical Treat

2 handfuls of spinach

2 carrots

1/4 chopped pineapple

1 handful of fresh or frozen mango

Water

Making It

Put all ingredients in your Nutri Ninja cup and blend.

Did You Know

Mango is a popular fruit (especially in my house!) It has some great health promoting attributes, including dietary fibre, vitamins, minerals and antioxidant compounds. Mango is rich in vitamin A and flavonoids, including beta-carotene which is great for healthy vision. The high dietary fibre content of mangoes make them a great ingredient to include in a weight loss smoothie.

The Easy Peasy

2 handfuls of romaine lettuce

2 handfuls of fresh or frozen mango

Water

Making It

Try and pick a crisp and fresh romaine lettuce to use in your smoothie. Place all ingredients into the Nutri Ninja and blend. Feel free to substitute the water for coconut water if you fancy changing it up a bit.

Did You Know

Romaine Lettuce is a great green leafy base to use in your smoothie. The flavour is quite mild in taste, making it great to use if you are trying to get used to the richer taste of other greens. Romaine lettuce contains all 9 essential amino acids, what a great nutritional boost to include in your smoothie. Romaine lettuce is high in calcium, omega-3 essential fats and has more vitamin A than a carrot! The water content of a romaine lettuce is high, making it perfect for keeping you hydrated whilst helping you lose weight. Despite not being one of the darker greens, romaine lettuce is still very rich in minerals. It is also high in iron. What's not to like?

Energy Boost Smoothies

No matter how healthy we are trying to be, we're eating all the right foods and getting more sleep, we all hit a point where we need an energy boost. For me, this is usually mid-afternoon. I used to get round this with a quick caffeine boost, or half a packet of biscuits. Needless to say, the boost was short lived. Unfortunately, the detrimental effect on my health was longer lasting.

If like me, an afternoon nap is out of the question, you'll need a quick and nutritious pick me up that doesn't involve a fake junk fix.

Smoothies can be the perfect solution. Using the Nutri Ninja makes it much easier to create an energy boosting smoothie in a short amount of time. If you are out at work or elsewhere when the slump hits, make up one of the following smoothies before you leave home and take it with you.

Feel the Beet

2 handfuls of romaine lettuce

1/2 raw beetroot

1 carrot

1/2 stick of celery

Half a lemon (if unwaxed you can leave the skin on)

Water

Ice cubes

Making It

How you use the raw beetroot will come down to your personal taste. I find it quite hard to take the earthy taste of a blended beetroot so I tend to pop mine in my juicer and use the juice to put in my Nutri Ninja. However, I know many others who love the taste so just put it straight in their blender. Adding lemon or lime juice can help mask the taste if you want to blend it for convenience. Put all the ingredients in your blender and mix until you have the desired consistency.

Did You Know

Beetroot has approximately 20 times the amount of nitrates as other vegetables. The nitrate converts into nitric oxide in our bodies which helps to provide us with longer lasting energy. Beetroot widens the blood vessels allowing oxygen to flow more easily, increasing your energy and stamina levels. Beetroot is also rich in iron, an essential mineral needed for healthy blood and energy production.

Vitamin Vrrrooom

1 handful of kale

1 handful of broccoli florets (can use frozen)

1 banana

250ml of coconut water

Ice cubes

Making It

Due to the high power of the Nutri Ninja it makes for a great machine for blending broccoli. You can use frozen broccoli if you prefer, and start with a few florets if you are not used to the taste. The banana in this recipe really helps to sweeten up the taste.

Place all the ingredients into the Nutri Ninja and blend.

Did You Know

Broccoli is full of dietary fibre, great for making you feel full up and controlling your blood sugar levels, creating longer lasting energy. Broccoli is a great source of beta-carotene, calcium, vitamin C, potassium, magnesium and vitamin B.

Go Bananas

---

2 handfuls of kale

1 apple

2 bananas

Water

Ice cubes

Making It

If you are able to use frozen bananas then it will negate the need for using ice cubes. If they are not frozen then fresh is fine. I either buy mine frozen (often as part of a mixed bag of frozen fruit) or I will chop them up and freeze them from fresh. Place all the ingredients in the Nutri Ninja and blend.

Did You Know

Bananas are the food of choice of Jamaican Olympic sprinter Yohan Blake. Apparently he scoffs 16 bananas a day! Personally, I probably wouldn't (and couldn't!) eat that many in a day, but he is right to get his energy the natural way. Bananas help to keep your blood sugar levels stable, the sucrose contain in a banana which acts more slowly than other sugars. So, you get the same energy high as you would get from a fizzy energy drink but without the crash afterwards. You'll find me on the running track.

Grape Vitality

2 handfuls of romaine lettuce

1 carrot

2 handful of grapes

1 table spoon of ground flaxseed

250ml of water

Making It

Place all the ingredients in your blender and blend until smooth. As with other ingredients you can freeze your grapes if you want and take them from the freezer as and when you need them.

Did You Know

Grapes are a great source of vitamin B1. Vitamin B1 is great for providing your body with a great energy boost. Plus, they taste great!

Plucky Peach

1 handful of spinach

2 peaches

1 handful of fresh or frozen mango

Water

Ice cubes

Making It

Place all the ingredients in your Nutri Ninja and blend. Feel free to substitute the water with coconut water or another healthy liquid (unsweetened nut milk etc.)

Did You Know

Peaches are a rich source of carbohydrates and natural sugars so great for an energy boost. If you use dried peaches they are also a great source of iron.

Oat Me Up

1 handful of romaine lettuce

1 handful of fresh or frozen mango

1 handful of oatmeal

Juice from 2 oranges

250ml coconut water

Ice cubes

Making It

Place all ingredients in the Nutri Ninja and blend. You might need to blend the ingredients for a little longer to ensure a smoother consistency with the oats. Or if you like a bit of crunch in your smoothie then blend for the usual 20-30 seconds.

Did You Know

Oatmeal is great for boosting energy. Oats are great for controlling blood sugar levels meaning your energy levels stay balanced. Oats are of course a great source of carbohydrates, perfect for your energy needs.

Sports Drinks

Whether it is before, during or after exercise it is really important to be filling your body with the right fuel. There are plenty of sports drinks available to buy, but not all are going to help your health long term. Personally, I find them quite sickly as they tend to be really sweet. I much prefer to make my own up.

The following smoothies are quick and easy to make with your blender, and will really help you perform to the best of your ability, and then aid in the recovery post exercise. I'm not promising to turn you into the next Usain Bolt, but it'll give you a fighting chance, reach for the stars right?!

The Beetroot Bolt

1 handful of kale

1 small raw beetroot (or use beetroot juice instead)

1 apple

1/4 pineapple

1/4 cucumber

Half a lime

250ml water

Ice

Making It

I mentioned this earlier in the book, the raw beetroot can either be blended or juiced, depending on your preferences (and of course if you have a juicer.) Place all the ingredients in your Nutri Ninja and blend.

Did You Know

The Power of Beetroot

When I trained for and ran my last marathon I used raw beetroot quite a bit. I even drunk it during the marathon event itself to help my body cope with the intensity of what it was going through.

According to research from Exeter University there are two marked physiological effects from beetroot juice. It contains high levels of nitrate which widens the blood vessels, reducing blood pressure and allowing more blood to flow. It cuts the amount of oxygen needed by muscles, making exercise less tiring.

"We were amazed by the effects of beetroot juice." Professor Andy Jones University of Exeter.

Beetroot juice has been one of the biggest stories in sports science after researchers at the

University of Exeter found it enables people to exercise for up to 16% longer.

The startling results have led to a host of athletes – from Premiership footballers to professional cyclists – looking into its potential uses.

It took some experimenting to get this smoothie tasting just right. Raw beetroot has a distinctive earthy taste to it which I really needed to figure out a way to disguise if I was going to be able to drink it mid run.

Top Tip

If you are drinking **The Beetroot Bolt** whilst running or doing any other sports, try and master the skill of keeping it all in your mouth. That is, don't let any dribble out. Due to the bright red blood like colour of beetroots, you will quite possibly attract some unnecessary attention from concerned people nearby. I talk from experience.

Cool as a Cucumber

1 handful of romaine lettuce

1 apple

1/2 cucumber

Half a lime

Water

Ice cubes

Making It

Put all the ingredients in your Nutri Ninja. Add water up to the max line or less if you prefer a thicker consistency.

Did You Know

The **cucumber** contains over 90% water, second only to the watermelon for it's high water content. This makes cucumber the ideal thirst quencher for not only hot days but for use during and after working out. If you can buy organic cucumbers, even better. This way you can blend the skin, which is where high quantities of silica is found. Silica is a mineral that helps strengthen tendons, muscles, cartilage, bones, ligaments and skin.

Walnut Wonder

1 apple

1 banana
1/4 cup of walnuts
1 handful of fresh or frozen raspberries

250ml of coconut water

Ice cubes

Making It

Place all the ingredients in the Nutri Ninja cup and blend. The sweetness of the raspberries and banana will mask the taste for anyone that has a dislike of walnuts.

Did You Know

Walnuts contain linolenic and linolenic fatty acid, two heart healthy essential fatty acids. Walnuts are also a great source of protein, fibre and are also high in magnesium and potassium, essential electrolytes for muscle function.

Build Me Up

1 handful of spinach

1 apple

2 bananas

4 tbsp wheatgerm

250ml of unsweetened almond milk/coconut water/water

Ice cubes

Making It

Wheatgerm can be bought at all good supermarkets, health food stores or online. Place all the ingredients in your Nutri Ninja blender. Feel free to substitute the almond milk for coconut water or plain water.

Did You Know

Wheatgerm is nutrient rich. It is high in essential fatty acids, vitamin B, amino acids and vitamin E. It is a brilliant source of energy and is said to increase stamina and performance. Wheatgerm is also a great source of protein which helps to maintain healthy muscles and regulate energy levels.

Melon Madness

2 handfuls of romaine lettuce

2 cups of seedless watermelon

1 handful of fresh or frozen strawberries

Water

Ice cubes (if not using frozen ingredients)

Making It

You won't need to include as much water in this recipe due to the high water content found in watermelons. Feel free to adjust the water levels accordingly. Place all the ingredients in the Nutri Ninja and blend. This is a smoothie perfect for hot summer days.

Did You Know

Watermelons don't contain as many nutrients as other fruits but they are high in beta-carotene and vitamin c. They also contain lycopene (the same nutrient found in tomatoes.) The high water content in watermelons make them a great ingredient to include in a smoothie to sip on to rehydrate during and after a workout.

Cashew Crazy

1 apple

1 handful of cashew nuts

2 bananas

1 tsp Spirulina

Water

Ice cubes

Making It

Place all of the ingredients in your Nutri Ninja and blend. Spirulina can be bought in all good health food shops and online. It is quite an acquired taste so you may want to get yourself used to it by starting with tiny amounts. It will also turn your smoothie a striking green colour.

Did You Know

Cashews contain monounsaturated fats which help promote good cardiovascular health. They are also great for great looking skin and hair.

Spirulina is often used by athletes as a nutritional supplement. Spirulina is a blue green algae that's been around for some 3 billion years. Spirulina is said to help protect athletes from the effects of overtraining and can help improve endurance. Spirulina helps the body to burn fat rather than carbs when working out, this allows the body to work out for longer as energy levels are kept higher.

Powered By...

2 handfuls of mixed greens (kale, spinach, romaine lettuce and any others you have)

1/2 avocado

1 handful of fresh or frozen raspberries

250ml of coconut water

Ice cubes

Making It

Get the benefits of all the greens in one go! Place all ingredients in the Nutri Ninja and blend.

Did You Know

Avocados are a superfood, worthy of the name. It is one of the healthiest foods you can consume in your diet. They are rich in monounsaturated fats making them a fabulous source of energy when you need to work out. I often have this smoothie a couple of hours before a long training run. In fact it is the very smoothie I drank before I completed a marathon.

Clearer and Younger Looking Skin Smoothies

You can spend all you want on expensive skin creams, if you are not nourishing your body from the inside, it will show on the outside. Eating the right foods will not only be cheaper than the latest skin cream, but you will also reap the benefits across your whole body.

The cells in your skin are constantly shedding and being replaced by younger ones. To support this speedy growth, you need to supply your skin with the right balance of nourishing foods. Fruit and vegetables help to protect the skin from cellular damage due to the powerful abundance of antioxidants that they contain.

Eating a wide range of colourful ingredients will help your skin become more supple, toned, smooth, younger looking and healthy. You will discover that once you are regularly feeding your body with the right foods, your skin will reward you with a blemish and spot free glow.

Essentials for Healthy Skin

- Water - Stay hydrated by drinking at least 8 cups of water a day. Your skin needs the moisture and hydration to look fresh and young. Even a little amount of dehydration will dry out your skin and make you look tired.

- Essential Fatty Acids - Found in nuts, seeds, avocados and fish. All these will help you skin to stay supple by acting as a natural moisturiser. With their high levels of vitamin E your skin will have a lovely supple look.

- Omega 3 and Omega 6 - These cannot be made in your body so need to be taken from your diet. They can be found in oily fish as well as flaxseed, linseeds and walnuts.

- Selenium - this powerful antioxidant, which can be found in tomatoes, Brazil Nuts, eggs and broccoli, are great for protecting against sun damage and age spots.

- Protect your skin in the sun from harmful rays

- Start your day with a glass of water with fresh lemon juice squeezed in it. Lemons contain a lot of vitamin C (as well as other antioxidants) which help reduce blemishes and wrinkles. Lemons are a great detoxifier, helping your body become cleaner on the inside, resulting in healthy and clear skin on the outside.

- Sleep - get more of it.

Blueberry Blast

1 bunch of parsley

1 handful of spinach

1/4 pineapple

2 handfuls of frozen blueberries

250ml of oatmilk

Ice cubes

Making It

Place all of the ingredients in the Nutri Ninja blender. Feel free to substitute the oat milk for an unsweetened nut milk or other healthy liquid alternative.

Did You Know

Eating **blueberries** can help leave your skin with a softer and younger look and feel. The antioxidants and phytochemicals found in blueberries help to neutralize free radicals which can damage skin cells. Due to the nutrients found in blueberries, they can assist with slowing down the aging process.

Parsley is very rich in calcium, iron and is a complete protein. Parsley is great for rejuvenating and detoxifying the body. It does have a distinctive taste and combines well with spinach. Studies show that parsley can help slow the aging process. Parsley is easy to grow at home too, how about that, really fresh parsley to pick as and when you need it.

Oat milk is high in natural fibre and iron and low in fat. Oats are also said to have properties within them that help with clearer skin by improving the health of it.

Clearer Cucumber

1 handful of spinach

1/2 cucumber

1 kiwi

250ml of coconut water

1 banana

Ice cubes

Making It

Peel the kiwi. Place all the ingredients in your Nutri Ninja and blend.

Did You Know

The skin of a **cucumber** contains the mineral silicia. Silica can be great for the complexion so is brilliant for people suffering with skin conditions. It also adds elasticity to your skin, great for creating younger looking skin, hooray for the cucumber!

Kiwis are high in vitamin E, an antioxidant known to protect skin from aging too quickly.

Brazilian Beauty

1 handful of spinach

1 banana

1 handful of fresh or frozen mango

3 Brazil nuts

1 tbsp ground flax seeds

250ml of coconut water or plain water

Making It

Put all the ingredients in the Nutri Ninja cup and blend. The Brazil nuts add a lovely creamy taste to the smoothie. Drink and pretend you're on the beaches of Rio.

Did You Know

Brazil nuts are packed full of nutrients. They have an abundance of vitamins, antioxidants and minerals. One important antioxidant mineral that the Brazil nut has a lot of is selenium.

Selenium helps maintain the elasticity and firmness of your skin. It can also help reduce sun damage.

Mango Tango

1 apple

1 banana

1 handful of fresh or frozen mango

250ml of coconut water or plain water

Ice cubes

Making It

Chop up the apple and banana. Add all the ingredients to the Nutri Ninja blender. Blend the ingredients. Add more liquid if you prefer a thinner consistency.

Did You Know

Mango contains vitamins B6, C and E, all of which help boost your skin. As mangoes are rich in beta-carotene it can help with acne and lack luster looking skin. Mango can of course also be used externally to help cleanse your skin. Personally, I rather eat it though!

Strawberry Sip

1 handful of spinach

1 handful of romaine lettuce

2 handfuls of fresh or frozen strawberries

1 tbsp of ground flaxseeds

250ml of water

Ice cubes

Making It

Add all the ingredients to the Nutri Ninja and blend.

Did You Know

Ground flaxseeds are plentiful in essential fatty acids which are brilliant for keeping your skin hydrated, soft and smooth looking. It is said that flax seeds may help reduce skin irritations and rashes.

Up the Apples & Pears

1 handfuls of spinach

1 handful of fresh or frozen blueberries

1 apple

1 pear

1 tbsp of ground flaxseeds

250ml of coconut water

Ice cubes

Making It

Add all the ingredients to the Nutri Ninja blender and top up with water if required. Blend for around 30 seconds or until smooth.

Did You Know

Apples are great for cleaning the colon and getting your skin looking clear. They are full of vitamin C which is fantastic for your skin complexion. Apples also contain vitamin Bs which are good for skin problems.

Pears are an anti-aging fruit that can really boost your skin's appearance and health. Pears contain a lot of fibre which is great for your skin. It helps to keep your complexion looking smooth.

Oooh Peachy

1 handful of kale

2 peaches

2 handfuls of grapes

250ml coconut water

Ice cubes

Making It

Place all the ingredients in your Nutri Ninja blender. Blend for approximately 30 seconds. Add more liquid if required.

Did You Know

Peaches contain vitamin C which is a major health benefit for the skin.

Grapes are a great source of flavonoids. Flavonoids are very powerful antioxidants that can help slow down aging. They have a high nutrient content which is important for a healthy body.

Cashew Crunch

1 handful of mixed greens

1/4 pineapple

1 handful of fresh or frozen strawberries

1 handful of cashew nuts

Water

Ice cubes

Making It

Remove the skin from the pineapple and chop. Place all the ingredients in the blender cup and blend for around 30 seconds.

Did You Know

Cashew nuts are rich in selenium and zinc. Selenium works alongside vitamin E which helps to hydrate the skin and reduce skin inflammation. Zinc is great for the immune

Superfood Smoothies

There is no legal or medical definition of what makes a food make it as a super food. In general though, they are foods that are found in nature and rich in nutrients. They are said to have certain health benefits which can help to combat certain ailments and reduce your risk of getting others.

system and cell growth, helping to renew skin that may have been damaged previously.

The Green Machine

1 handful of spinach

1 handful of kale

1/2 avocado

1/4 cucumber

Juice of 1 lime

250ml of coconut water

Ice cubes

Making It

Scoop out the flesh of the avocado. Squeeze the juice from 1 lime. Add all the other ingredients. Add more water if required. Blend for 30 seconds or until smooth.

I love this smoothie. The combination of all the green goodness makes me feel like my body is really getting all the nutrients I need. Individually they are all ingredients I wouldn't really eat, but combined in a smoothie like this I love them.

Purple Punch

1 handful of romaine lettuce

250ml frozen mixed berries

1/2 tsp cinnamon

125ml pomegranate juice

50ml of probiotic vanilla yoghurt

Water

Making It

Place all the ingredients in the blender. Blend for 30 seconds. Add water if you want a thinner consistency.

Did You Know

The **pomegranate** and in particular, pomegranate juice, has remarkable levels of antioxidant properties. Pomegranates are abundantly rich in potassium, fibre, vitamin C, niacin and disease fighting antioxidants.

Top Tip

You could pour the juice into ice cube trays and freeze. The perfect way to get your smoothie super cold and tasty whilst including a superfood.

Cinnamon equals Christmas memories for me, so a welcome addition to any smoothie. Memories aside, cinnamon helps to balance blood sugar levels.

Blueberry Beauties

1 handful of kale

1/2 banana

2 handful of fresh or frozen blueberries

250ml unsweetened almond milk

Ice cubes

Making It

Add all of the ingredients to the Nutri Ninja Blender. If you don't like almond milk feel free to substitute it for coconut water or just plain water. Blend for 30 seconds.

Did You Know

Blueberries are a popular superfood. They are high in numerous vitamins and minerals. They help slow down the signs of ageing. They contain high levels of antioxidants which are said to help protect against many health issues, including heart disease, stroke, gum disease amongst others. They are also reported as helping to enhance eyesight.

Kale Crunch

2 handfuls of kale

1/2 pineapple

1/2 banana

250ml coconut water

Ice cubes

Making It

Place all the ingredients in the Nutri Ninja and blend. Add more coconut water or plain water if required. Blend for around 30 seconds or until smooth.

Did You Know

Kale contains all the essential amino acids and 9 non essential ones. It has an exceptionally high level of protein in it and is a powerful antioxidant.

Oat-tastic

1 pear

1 apple

30g oatmeal

1 tbsp honey

250ml of unsweetened almond milk

Ice cubes

Making It

Chop the apple and pear up, removing the core, leaving the skin on. Add the other ingredients and top up with water if required. Blend for about 30 seconds until smooth.

Did You Know

Oats are a traditional remedy for helping with digestive problems. They are highly nutritious being a good source of protein and high in calcium, potassium and magnesium. They provide us with sustainable energy and make for a fantastic filling addition to any smoothie.

Hey Honey

1 handful of romaine lettuce

1 handful of watercress

1 tbsp of honey

1 handful of fresh or frozen blueberries

1 tbsp of chia seeds

250ml of coconut water

Ice cubes

Making It

Add all of the ingredients to your Nutri Ninja. Add more water if required. Blend for around 30 seconds or until smooth.

Did You Know

Winnie Pooh was on to something with his love of honey. **Honey** is a powerful addition to your daily diet. This isn't a new finding - the health benefits of honey go back to early Greek, Roman, Vedic and Islamic texts. The list of healing properties and benefits of honey is a book all in itself, there are countless reports and studies to show that honey is a powerhouse of nutrients that can help soothe coughs, boost memory, help with allergies and plenty more.

Watercress is great for vitamin deficiencies and makes a tasty addition to any smoothie. When eaten raw, watercress is a rich source of minerals and vitamins. It contains an abundance of vitamin K and vitamin A which are great for your bones and eye well being. Watercress also has high levels of antioxidants.

Go Nuts

1 handful of spinach

1 handful of mixed nuts (try a variety but definitely include walnuts)

1/2 banana

250ml of coconut water

Ice cubes

Making It

Add all the ingredients. Top up with water if required. Blend for around 30 seconds or until smooth.

Did You Know

Walnuts are a rich source of omega-3 fatty acids. They are also a good source of fibre and protein. Walnuts are the golden star of nuts with the highest overall antioxidant activity of them all.

The Blackberry

1 stick of celery

1 handful of fresh or frozen blackberries

2 kiwis

Half a lemon (unwaxed)

250ml coconut water

Making It

Chop the ingredients and place them all in the blender. Blend for 30 seconds.

Did You Know

Blackberries have a high concentration of antioxidants. They are low in calories, high in fibre and rich in nutrients. They have a lot of fibre and are almost fat free, making them a perfect addition for a healthy smoothie. Blackberries has folic acid and vitamins C and K, all which are great for your joints and bones. Plus they taste great!

Easy Squeezy

1 handful of spinach

2 apples

1/2 lemon (unwaxed)

Water

Ice Cubes

Making It

Chop apples. If you are not using an unwaxed lemon make sure you peel it. Add all ingredients and top up with the desired amount of water. Blend for around 30 seconds or until smooth.

Did You Know

Studies have shown that eating an apple a day can lower bad cholesterol in the blood. **Apples** contain polyphenol antioxidants which are said to lower blood oxidation.

Lemon juice is a great alkalizer for the body. Did you know when we have too much acid in our body our energy levels drop and our immune systems do not work at their full ability? Lemon is said to be great at detoxing your body.

A great drink that I have grown to love is hot water with the juice of half a lemon. It is meant to improve liver function and help eliminate kidney stones.

Healthy Heart Smoothies

Getting regular exercise combined with eating nutrient rich healthy food is something your heart will love you for. And a happy heart is a healthy heart. Eating a well-balanced diet rich in fruits and vegetables will ensure that your risk of developing heart disease is significantly reduced. The more nutrients and healthy fats that you consume, the better. Drinking a smoothie a day will go a long way to making this possible. You can make sure that your heart is getting all the fibre it needs whilst ensuring your cholesterol stays low.

Flaxseed, oatmeal, walnuts, soy milk, blueberries, carrots, spinach, broccoli, dark chocolate (lowers blood pressure.)

Heart Beet

1 handful of kale

1/2 beetroot

1 apple

1 carrot

1/2 lemon (unwaxed)

1 table spoon of ground flaxseed

Water

Ice cubes

Making It

As mentioned elsewhere in this book, beetroot can have a powerful taste. If you find it too strong please feel free to juice the beetroot or use a lower quantity. Add all the ingredients into the Nutri Ninja cup. Top up with water. Blend for around 30 seconds or until smooth.

Did You Know

Beetroot is a powerful blood cleanser and tonic. Beetroot promotes a healthy digestive system as well as a healthy heart. Beetroot is a great blood builder and fortifier.

Avocado Baby

1 handful of mixed greens

1/2 ripe avocado

1/2 banana

1 handful of fresh or frozen strawberries

Water

Ice cubes

Making It

Scoop out the flesh of the avocado. Add all the ingredients to the Nutri Ninja blender cup. Top up with water or other liquid. Blend for around 30 seconds.

Did You Know

Avocados can aid in lowering our risk of heart disease due to their monounsaturated fatty acid content. The vitamin B-6 and folic acid also plays a part in supporting a healthy heart.

I Heart Chocolate

1 handful of spinach

1 handful of frozen raspberries

1 banana

2 squares of grated dark chocolate (minimum 75% cocoa content)

1 table spoon of peanut butter (natural if possible)

250ml of coconut water

Ice cubes

Making It

Grate the chocolate. Place all the ingredients in the blender cup and blend for about 30 seconds. Add more liquid if you require a thinner drink.

Did You Know

Studies show that **dark chocolate** can help lower your blood pressure. By eating good quality dark chocolate a few times a week you can help prevent the formation of blood clots along with improve the blood flow to your heart.

Peanut butter (if of the natural variety) has around 75% unsaturated fats which helps keep your heart healthy. The protein and fat in natural peanut butter will keep you feeling fuller for longer.

Acai Heart

1 handful of mixed greens

1 tbsp of acai berries (fresh, dried or powdered)

1 handful of fresh or frozen blueberries

250ml of soy milk/unsweetened nut milk

Ice cubes

Making It

Add all the ingredients to the Nutri Ninja cup and blend. Top up with water if required. Acai berries can be purchased from some supermarkets and all health food stores.

Did You Know

Commonly found in the rain forests of the Amazon, **acai berries** are very high in antioxidants. They are said to help prevent blood clots by improving overall blood circulation and relaxing the blood vessels.

Heart Healthy Super Greens

1 handful of spinach

1 handful of kale

1 apple

1 carrot

1 tbsp of mixed seeds

250ml of coconut Water

Ice cubes

Making It

Add all the ingredients to the blender. Feel free to add more seeds if you wish. Top up with water if required. Blend for around 30 seconds.

Did You Know

You will probably have seen spinach and kale feature quite heavily throughout this book, and with good reason. They are both so incredibly good for you, with so many health benefits. **Kale** can help lower cholesterol levels. Kale is low in calories, high in fibre and has zero fat. **Spinach** has high levels of potassium and low levels of sodium, the composition of these minerals helps to lower blood pressure.

Smoothie Remedies

It is always worth looking at your diet when you start suffering from some common ailments. If our bodies are lacking in nutrients we can help ourselves by consuming the right foods.

By making a few simple lifestyle changes and implementing particular foods into our diet we can help protect and promote vibrant health.

Eating raw foods when combined with exercise, rest and the right attitude can go a long way to making you feel better and less reliant on quick fixes.

(If you are taking medication please remember to consult a doctor before making any decisions about stopping them.)

The Anti-Sneeze

1 apple

1/2 pineapple

1cm ginger

1/2 lemon (unwaxed)

1 tbsp of honey

Water

Ice cubes

Making It

Peel the pineapple and chop. Peel the skin from the lemon if you are using the unwaxed variety. Add all ingredients to the blender. Top up with water. Blend for around 30 seconds.

Did You Know

If you suffer from hay fever you will know the frustrations of sneezing and feeling blocked up, amongst other ailments. Consuming the combination of these ingredients may go some way to giving you some relief. Pineapple contains bromeline which is an enzyme that can aid in dissolving excess mucus. Ginger is a natural decongestant and honey has been said to help fight off the symptoms of hayfever, especially if you are using a locally produced honey.

Abundantly Rich Smoothie

1 handful of spinach

1 handful of kale

1 handful of fresh or frozen blueberries

1 apple

1 tbsp ground flaxseeds

1 tbsp of honey

Water

Ice cubes

Making It

Add all the ingredients to the Nutri Ninja blender. Top up with water. Blend for around 30 seconds.

Did You Know

You can add a tablespoon of **ground flaxseeds** to any smoothie (but don't have more than 2 tablespoons in a day as the husks contain compounds that can be toxic in high doses.) The amazing health giving properties of flaxseed are recognized around the world. They are a rich source of dietary fibre which can help relieve constipation. Other benefits include essential fatty acids, in particular omega 3 and omega 6.

Cause I Eats Me Spinach

2 handfuls of spinach

1 carrot

3 ready to eat dried apricots

1/2 lemon (unwaxed)

250ml coconut water

Ice cubes

Making It

Place all the ingredients in the Nutri Ninja blender. Add more water or liquid if required.

Did You Know

Popeye had the right idea. **Spinach** is one of the healthiest foods you can eat. Spinach is one of the best sources of folate which is necessary for brain and cardiovascular health. If you suffer from anemia as a result of low iron levels, spinach is a fantastic remedy, containing nearly twice as much iron as most other greens.

Dried apricots are another great source of iron, meaning the combination of these two iron rich foods in one smoothie will do wonders for your iron, and in turn, energy levels.

Going Back to Your Roots

1 handful of romaine lettuce

1/2 raw beetroot

1 carrot

1cm of ginger

1/2 lemon (unwaxed)

Water

Ice cubes

Making It

Add all the ingredients to the Nutri Ninja. If you don't like the strong taste of raw beetroot you may want to juice it instead. Add more water or liquid if required.

Did You Know

Beetroot has many amazing health benefits. It is great for cleansing the liver, increasing iron levels and helping lower blood pressure.

Winter Booster

1 apple

Juice from 2 oranges

2 passion fruits

1 handful of fresh or frozen mango

Half a lemon (unwaxed)

1 tsp of echinacea powder

Water

Ice cubes

Making It

Chop the apple. You can add the whole oranges (peeled) if you prefer. Scoop out the pulp of the passion fruits. Add all ingredients to the Nutri Ninja and top up with water. Blend for around 30 seconds. Echinacea can be bought from any health store or ordered online. Passion fruits are best when they are ripe.

Did You Know

This is the perfect smoothie to fight off cold and flu. Echinacea, mango, pineapple and oranges are all rich in vitamin C

The Pick Me Up

1 handful of spinach

1 apple

1 orange

1 tbsp honey

1cm of fresh root ginger

1 handful of fresh or frozen mango

1/4 pineapple

250ml of coconut water

Ice cubes

Making It

There is quite a lot to squeeze into this smoothie. I made this recently for my son when he was feeling run down after a bout of a winter cold virus. He loved the taste of it and it really did perk him up. Chop the apple, peel the orange (if you don't like bits, juice it instead.) Peel the pineapple and chop it up. Blend everything together.

Did You Know

When you are feeling run down a smoothie is a quick way to get a lot of vitamins and nutrients into your system. All of these ingredients are great for boosting your immune system due to the amount of vitamin C present. The pineapple can help dissolve excess mucus so particularly good when you have a cold.

Prune Relief

2 handfuls of kale

1 banana

1 pear

3 dried prunes (pitted)

250ml water

Ice cubes

Making It

Place all the ingredients in the blender. You may want to blend for a bit longer than the 30 seconds if the prunes haven't quite got to a smooth enough consistency.

Did You Know

Prunes are the most natural laxative you can get. If you struggle with constipation then the combination of the prunes with the soluble fibre of the apples and pears, will have you relieved soon enough. Prunes are also a brilliant source of beta carotene and vitamin K.

Ginger Zest

2 carrots

1 handful of fresh or frozen mango

1/4 cucumber

1cm ginger

1/2 lemon (unwaxed)

Water

Ice cubes

Making It

Add all the ingredients to the Nutri Ninja. If you are not using unwaxed lemons, peel the skin off and just add the flesh. Top up with water. Blend for around 30 seconds.

Did You Know

Fresh root ginger is a fantastic natural cure for unsettled stomachs and indigestion. It is a natural antibiotic and decongestant. Ginger is also warming and soothing and a favourite natural remedy for colds.

Breakfast Smoothies

It's been said many times before, breakfast is the most important meal of the day. If I ever skip breakfast I start to feel *really* hungry by 10am. This is when I'm at my weakest, when I'm really hungry, and I find myself reaching for a quick fix, often unhealthy, energy boost.

By incorporating a smoothie into your breakfast routine, you will be setting yourself up for a healthy and productive day, filling your body up with nature's finest fuel. Make extra so that you can sip on some mid-morning.

Sometimes I will just have a smoothie for breakfast, depending on how I am feeling and what I am doing. I quite often go for a run in the morning, so it makes sense for me to just have a smoothie. I find it helpful to plan the night before what smoothie I am going to have, that way I have no excuse to skip it when I am in a rush in the morning.

Rocket Boost

1 handful of fresh or frozen raspberries

1 handful of fresh or frozen blueberries

200ml oat milk

3 tablespoons of live natural yoghurt

1 tablespoon of honey

Making It

Place all of the ingredients in the Nutri Ninja cup and blend for 30 seconds. Top up with water or more oat milk if required. If you don't like yoghurt then feel free to add less or leave it out altogether.

Did You Know

Oat milk is made with presoaked oat groats (hulled grains broken down.) Oat milk has a slightly sweet but mild taste. It makes for a great substitute for milk. It is very low in fat and is lactose free. It makes for a great vegan alternative. Oatmilk contains 15 vitamins and 10 minerals. It has more vitamin A than cow's milk. It is also high in iron so great for any anemia sufferers out there.

Berry Tasty

1 large apple

1 handful of fresh or frozen raspberries

1 handful of fresh or frozen strawberries

1 orange (or the juice of one)

250ml coconut water

Ice cubes

Making It

Chop up the apple, removing the core. Add all the ingredients to the Nutri Ninja blender. Top up with more water if required. Blend for 30 seconds or until smooth.

Did You Know

Berries make a brilliant start to the day and feel like quite a treat. They are a great way of getting antioxidants and phtonutrients into your system. They are great for your immune system and disease fighting abilities. Don't underestimate the power of the berries.

Filling Breakfast Smoothie

1 pear

1 banana

50g muesli

1 tbsp natural maple syrup

200ml unsweetened soy milk

Making It

Chop the pear and add all the ingredients to your Nutri Ninja. Top up with water if required. Blend for 30 seconds or until smooth.

Did You Know

Maple Syrup can boost your immune system, sooth your stomach and help ageing skin. When you buy maple syrup make sure that 'maple syrup' is the only ingredient listed. It is loaded with antioxidants in the form of polyphenols.

Maple syrup also contains essential nutrients like zinc and manganese. Zinc is great for resisting illness and manganese helps protect immune cells from damage.

Kicking K

3 kiwis

2 stick celery

1 banana

Water

Ice Cubes

Making It

Place all ingredients in the cup, fill with water up to the max line. If you prefer a thicker smoothie substitute the water for unsweetened almond milk, oat milk, or another healthy liquid alternative.

Did You Know

Kiwis are a very nutrient rich fruit containing vitamins C, E and beta-carotene. They are full of healthy minerals including calcium, magnesium, phosphorus, potassium and sodium. They are great for providing you with an energy boost to start the day. The high vitamin C content will help strengthen your immune system too.

Great Greens

1 handful of spinach

1 handful of kale

1/4 cucumber

1/4 medium pineapple

1/2 ripe avocado

250ml coconut water

Ice cubes

Making It

Scoop out the flesh from a ripe avocado. Place all ingredients in the Nutri Ninja and blend. Add more liquid if required.

Did You Know

Avocados are a great way to set you up for a healthy day. They contain all the vital vitamins, minerals and fats required to keep you in peak condition. They are filling (in a good way) so will keep you feeling fuller for longer.

Smoothies for Kids

It feels really great to know that not only myself, but the children too, are getting their full recommendation of vitamins and nutrients, in the healthiest style, before they've even left for school in the morning. Not only that, they are enjoying it too.

Don't get me wrong, we are not replacing the children's meals with smoothies. We still serve up an array of vegetables with their evening meals, but if there is the odd day they don't feel like eating them, I don't feel like I need to do battle with them to eat those last few peas they've cunningly hidden under their spoon. I know that they have already fuelled their bodies with nutrients from the best possible sources. The extras at mealtimes are the icing on the cake, so to speak.

These smoothies are not exclusively for the kiddies though. You'll reap the rewards of drinking them too. Allow your children to be really involved in the process - from choosing the recipe, picking up the ingredients and then making the smoothie. Discuss with them what nutrients are in each smoothie and what brilliance they are doing for their bodies. It sets them up for fantastic healthy habits for both now and adulthood.

Don't forget you can turn many of these smoothies into yummy and nutritious ice lollies.

Captain Bright Eye

3 medium carrots

1cm of ginger

Juice from 2 oranges

250ml of coconut water (or plain water)

Ice cubes

Making It

Add all the ingredients to the Nutri Ninja Blender. You may want to start with small amounts of ginger if your child isn't used to the taste. Just grate a little bit in and build up according to taste.

Did You Know

Carrots are naturally sweet, making them an excellent vegetable to include in a kid's smoothie. They are high in fibre and carotenoids.

But can they really make you see in the dark? Or was that just a ploy to get us, as children ourselves, to eat up all our carrots? Well, actually, there is some truth in it. They contain a lot of Vitamin A which helps you to produce rhodopsin. Rhodopsin is a purple pigment that your eyes need in order to see in dim light. So although you won't have quite the superpowers of night vision that you were led to believe, you will be able to see in some lights.

Strawberry Surprise

1 handful of spinach

2 handfuls of fresh or frozen strawberries

1 orange

Water

Ice cubes

Making It

Peel the orange and put segments into the blender. Add all the other ingredients and fill the water up to the max line. If you or your little one isn't keen on 'bits' then feel free to squeeze the juice out of the orange instead of putting the whole fruit in.

Did You Know

Strawberries are a fantastic source of vitamin C. Weight for weight they have more vitamin C than an orange. The seeds in strawberries provide fibre which helps with constipation.

Gone Bananas

1 handful of kale

1 handful of fresh or frozen strawberries

1 banana

250ml of coconut water (or other liquid to thin)

Ice cubes

Making It

Place all the ingredients in the Nutri Ninja and blend. Add more banana or strawberries if you prefer a thicker smoothie.

Did You Know

Bananas are great for an energy pick me up (as if the little monkeys ever require more energy!) and can make you feel less tired. Bananas are very high in potassium, an electrolyte that is vital for your body's function. Potassium helps to build proteins and maintain normal body growth. Bananas mixed with strawberries make a delicious combination.

Fruitylicious

Juice from 2 oranges

2 kiwis

1 Pear

Water

Ice cubes

Making It

Juice 2 orange, or if you don't mind bits just put the whole orange in the blender (without the skin.) Peel and cut the kiwis. Chop the pear up but leave the skin on. Add all the ingredients. Top up with water. Blend for about 30 seconds.

Peany B Booster

1 handful of spinach

1 tablespoon of peanut butter (natural if possible)

1 ripe banana

250ml unsweetened soy milk or an alternative recommended liquid.

Ice cubes

Making It

Place all of the ingredients in the Nutri Ninja and blend. If you can use a natural type of peanut butter even better. The regular peanut butter tends to have additives, preservatives, added sugar and salt.

Did You Know

Peanut butter is a staple in our household. Natural peanut butter should just have peanuts and salt listed as the ingredients. Peanut butter has potassium and protein in it together with fibre, healthy fats, vitamin E, antioxidants and plenty of magnesium to make your bones and muscles strong.

Mango Mayhem

1 handful of fresh or frozen mango

1/4 pineapple

1 apple

1/2 cucumber

250ml of coconut water (or water)

Ice cubes

Making It

Remove the skin from the pineapple and chop. Place all the ingredients into the blender. Add more water or liquid if you require a thinner consistency.

Did You Know

Mango is great for stimulating the immune system. It is a fantastic source of vitamins C and A as well as potassium. Kids love the taste of mango, it creates a deliciously smooth and tasty smoothie.

Super Green Machine

1 handful of spinach

1 handful of romaine lettuce

1 apple

1/2 ripe avocado

Half lime

1 tsp of honey

Water

Ice cubes

Making It

Chop the apple up. Scoop the avocado out of the skin. Add all the ingredients into the Nutri Ninja and fill with water to the max line. Blend for 30 seconds. Add more water if you prefer a thinner drink.

Did You Know

Avocado is perfect for ensuring your child is getting a balanced and nutritious diet. They are packed full of a 6 requirements for a healthy body: fat, protein, water, natural sugar, minerals and vitamins. Avocados are a great source of essential natural fats, the kind children need daily in their diet.

The Chocolate Monster

1 banana

2 squares of 75% cocoa content chocolate, grated

1 handful of frozen or fresh strawberries

250ml of coconut water

Ice cubes

Making It

Grate the chocolate. Place all the ingredients in the blender. Add more water if required. Add another banana or maybe even a scoop of yoghurt or vanilla ice cream to turn this into a tasty dessert.

The Secret Super Booster

2 broccoli florets

1 apple

1 carrot

1 handful of frozen strawberries

250ml of water

Making It

Put all ingredients in blender. Add more water if needed.

Did You Know

We keep on telling them how good broccoli is. If they don't believe you maybe a few of these smoothies will change their minds. Broccoli is a really important ingredient for a healthy diet. Broccoli has oodles of antibacterial and antiviral nutrients. It also has almost as much calcium as milk. Perfect for growing children. What's more, broccoli has almost twice as much protein as steak - who'd have thought it?

Peachy Lemonade

1 apple

2 peaches

Juice of half a lemon

100ml of coconut water

150ml of carbonated water (or you may know it as sparkling water)

Ice cubes

Making It

Place all the ingredients in the Nutri Ninja apart from the carbonated water. Blend. Add carbonated water to turn this delicious drink into lemonade, but not as they know it.

Did You Know

Peaches are a rich source of beta carotene which can be great vision health. Peaches have a wide range of vitamins and minerals. Peaches are also fibrous which is great for digestion and preventing constipation.

Thanks for Reading

I really hope that you have enjoyed the recipes in this book. I encourage you to test them out and get experimenting. If you don't have a certain ingredient available just leave it out or substitute it with another one. The idea of these smoothies is to get lots of incredible raw energy inside you every day, and have fun at the same time.

If you have found this book useful I would ***really*** appreciate it if you could spare a moment please to leave a review on Amazon.

It really helps and encourages me to keep on creating books. If you have any suggestions or questions please do feel free to get in contact with me at katelianagreen@hotmail.com.

If you have any smoothie recipe suggestions too,
I would love to hear from you too!

Happy blending.